INSTANT CHRISTMAS PAGEANT

Wee Three Kings

by
Marian Hope Moreland
and
Richard Moreland

Group
Loveland, Colorado

Instant Christmas Pageant:
WEE THREE KINGS

Copyright © 1999 Marian Hope Moreland and Richard Moreland

Visit our Web site: www.grouppublishing.com

Credits
Editor: Janis Sampson
Creative Development Editor: Paul Woods
Chief Creative Officer: Joani Schultz
Copy Editor: Shirley Michaels
Art Director: Ragont Design
Illustrator: Megan Jeffery
Cover Art Director: Lisa Chandler
Cover Illustrator: Kelly Cottrell
Cover Designer: Becky Hawley
Production Manager: Peggy Naylor
Audio Producer: Steve Saavedra

ISBN: 0-7644-2149-2

Printed in the United States of America.

INSTANT CHRISTMAS PAGEANT

WEE THREE KINGS
Contents

HOW TO USE THIS
Pageant

Bravo! Most of the preparation for your children's Christmas pageant is already done!

Instant Christmas Pageant: Wee Three Kings provides a complete Christmas program on compact disc. All the spoken dialogue, sound effects, and music are prerecorded. This book includes suggested pantomime actions, patterns, costume and prop ideas, publicity clip art, and pageant guidelines. Christmas hymns are here, too, so the audience gets to sing along, joining the children in praise to God.

Wee Three Kings is flexible and can be enjoyed by audiences in a variety of settings:

- a Sunday morning worship service,
- a family evening program,
- a community-wide matinee,
- a nursing home program,
- a Sunday school special event, or
- a children's puppet show.

Wee Three Kings is easy to prepare for, too. Just follow these simple steps:

1. Read this book cover to cover. (It won't take you very long.) While reading the script, listen to the CD.

2. Adjust the number of roles in the pageant to match the number of children who will be in your program. Check out how to vary the number of roles on page 6.

3. Play the CD for the children, and then assign parts.

4. Have kids help you collect and create costumes and props. Many props can be collected from your church or from kids' homes.

5. Ask kids for ideas to determine the best time and place for the pageant. The suggested props and costumes are portable, so children can perform the play for any number of audiences.

4

6. Have children help publicize the pageant. They can use the photocopiable clip art in this book (pp. 16-17) or the computer clip art on the CD. Simply put the CD into any Macintosh- or IBM-compatible CD-ROM drive, and read the instructions in the "Read Me" file. Let kids print out the clip art to use on fliers, bulletins, and posters. Children can decorate the posters using art and craft supplies and even send e-mail messages to family members, neighbors, and school friends.

7. Practice the play with the children. Remember: Kids don't have to memorize their lines! They don't have to lip-sync the parts either. Instead, they can "ham it up" by following the action instructions provided in the script. They can even supplement the script with actions of their own. After a few times through, kids will easily pantomime this action-packed drama.

8. Perform the play. Have a cast member or adult volunteer introduce the pageant and let the audience know they are welcome to sing along during the pageant. The same person could also lead the audience in singing each Christmas hymn.

It's that simple!

Here are a few additional suggestions to help you achieve an outstanding performance:

● To familiarize children with the Bible story, invite them to read and discuss with you Luke 2:1-20 and Matthew 2:1-12. Begin and end rehearsal times with prayer.

● Refer to the CD icon (see margin) to find exactly where a CD selection occurs in the pageant. Kids can easily practice their actions for a particular segment of the script with the corresponding CD track.

● Refer to the spotlight icon (see margin) for suggested lighting changes. If a spotlight is not available, be sure children understand that when their scene is not "in the spotlight," they should freeze their action.

● Before the performance, have children practice the actions and movements a few times so they feel comfortable with their roles.

● Because performance areas vary, you may have to pause the CD during the play to allow time for the kids to perform all their actions and movements.

● Invite teens and senior adults to assist children in producing the pageant. They can help as actors, directors, stage managers, prop handlers, costumers, and publicity agents.

CREATING THE
Characters

One of the best features of *Wee Three Kings* is that any child in your church can play almost any role. Since the spoken parts are prerecorded and kids don't have to memorize lines, younger children can play the main characters as easily as older children can. The Jester, Herald, Servants, Courtiers, and Scribes can be either male or female. The animals can be played by younger children.

If you have fewer than thirty-two children, combine the roles of Scribe 1 and Scribe 2. Pantomime characters, except for Mary and Joseph, could double as Scribes or Courtiers. Or teenagers and adults could help out by playing any of the adult roles.

If you have more than thirty-two children, you can increase the numbers of Servants, Courtiers, Angels, and animals. Or you can form a children's choir to lead the audience in singing the Christmas hymns.

Costume elements and props are suggested for each character. Be sure to check out the photocopiable patterns and instructions beginning on page 10.

CAST

Ernie—*Intelligent, well-mannered boy who knows a lot about the Bible.*
  Suggested costume: favorite team T-shirt, jeans, and sneakers. Midway through the pageant, he will need a Bible-times tunic to put on over his clothes.

Gert—*Ernie's older sister. She is bossy and willful and programs their time machine to carry them back in time.*
  Suggested costume: T-shirt, jeans, and sneakers. Midway through the pageant, she will need a Bible-times tunic to put on over her clothes.

Caleb—*Slave in the court of King Herod. He takes pride in his position.*
    Suggested costume: a simple bathrobe or sleeveless tunic and sandals. On one upper arm, he wears a gold or silver armband.

Rachel—*Caleb's younger sister. Quiet and thoughtful, she is also a slave in Herod's court.*
    Suggested costume: similar to Caleb's. She too wears an armband.

Servants (including Servants 1, 2, and 3)—*Workers in King Herod's court.*
    Suggested costume: similar to Caleb's. All wear armbands.

Ahab—*Overseer of servants in Herod's court. He is demanding and gruff.*
    Suggested costume: a bathrobe or tunic similar to Caleb's, but more colorful. He wears a double armband to distinguish his rank.

Jester—*Comic figure with a sock puppet on one hand.*
    Suggested costume: dark-colored bathrobe and sandals. A dark scarf is wrapped around his or her head so only the eyes are showing.

Yuk—*Sarcastic and insulting sock puppet worn on Jester's hand.*
    Suggested costume: bright yellow or red sock with simple face drawn on.

Roman Soldier—*Rough but dignified. Stands and walks with authority.*
    Suggested costume: a knee-length tunic; helmet; and dark, heavy sandals. A plastic sword in a sheath can be added. Attach the sheath to a cord, and put it over one shoulder with the sheath resting on one hip.

Mary and Joseph—*Jesus' earthly parents. Respected as honest and hardworking.*
    Suggested costume: bathrobes, sandals, and headdresses. May be draped in colorful scarves or sheets.

Donkey—*Lives in the stable where Jesus is born.*
    Suggested costume: gray or brown sweat pants, shirt, and socks.

Shepherds—*Sent by the Angel of the Lord to Bethlehem where Jesus is born.*
    Suggested costume: headdresses (a towel placed over each shepherd's head with a tie to secure the towel); bathrobes; sandals; and long staffs made from wooden dowels, canes, or large sticks.

Sheep—*Companions of the shepherds.*
   Suggested costume: white sweat pants, shirt, and socks.

Angel of the Lord—*Messenger of God who announces Jesus' birth to the shepherds.*
   Suggested costume: white sweat pants or slacks, white long-sleeve shirt, white socks, white sandals, and white sheet draped around the shoulders.

Angels—*Messengers of God who appear to shepherds in the field and glorify God.*
   Suggested costume: similar to Angel of the Lord's.

King Herod—*Sly and treacherous, a powerful but heartless ruler of Judea.*
   Suggested costume: crown, brightly colored robe (possibly purple or gold), and sandals. He also wears jewelry, such as gold neck chains and rings.

Courtiers—*Assistants to King Herod.*
   Suggested costume: robes and sandals, but no armbands.

Herald—*Herod's assistant who announces arriving visitors.*
   Suggested costume: similar to Caleb's.

Caspar—*One of three Wise Men seeking Jesus. Walks proudly and carries himself with dignity.*
   Suggested costume: crown, colorful robe, tunic, and sandals. Add ornate necklaces, rings, or bracelets.

Melchior—*Astronomer and scholar, similar to Caspar.*
   Suggested costume: similar to Caspar's.

Balthazar—*One of three Wise Men. An eccentric astronomer who has an unusual way of wording things.*
   Suggested costume: similar to Caspar's, with a few zany touches.

Scribes 1 and 2—*Herod's readers and record-keepers. Intimidated by him.*
   Suggested costume: similar to Courtiers'. They might carry feather quill pens.

Old Scribe—*Old and wise, he walks bent over. He knows and loves the Holy Scriptures.*
   Suggested costume: similar to Courtiers', with a beard added.

PREPARING THE
Costumes and Props

You can create many of the costumes, accessories, and props for *Wee Three Kings* using the instructions and patterns on the following pages. The patterns are photocopiable so you can distribute them to your kids and adult helpers.

In addition to costumes, accessories, and props, you'll need the following items:

● A CD player and the *Wee Three Kings* CD.

● A spotlight (optional).

● A trouble light or a bright flashlight.

● Four scrolls—one for the Roman Soldier and one for each of the Scribes.

● A large chair with arms draped with a rich-looking cloth to be Herod's throne.

● Three blankets, one for each of the Wise Men.

● Two dolls—one to be the baby Jesus in the manger, with a small blanket for swaddling cloths, and a larger doll with a blanket for Mary to hold in her arms during the Wise Men's visit.

● A crate or a box to use as a rustic-looking manger.

● A small wooden stool for Mary to sit on beside the manger.

● A simple wooden chair, a small wooden table with a simple vase of flowers, and a star for the house scene.

● Three gifts for the Wise Men to present to Jesus.

INSTRUCTIONS AND PATTERNS

Time Machine

Paint a large appliance crate silver, or cover it with silver foil. Place a flashlight inside the box to simulate light coming from within the machine. To simulate smoke, use dry ice in a shallow pan of water. Be sure to choose an adult, not a child, to carry the pan of dry ice on and off the stage.

Armbands

Using a tube from a paper towel or bathroom tissue roll, cut two-inch cylinders. Cut vertically through the cylinder so that the cut sides spring apart. The resulting C-shaped band should fit around a child's upper arm. Cover the armband with aluminum foil or shiny gold wrapping paper.

Yuk

Yuk, the Jester's sock puppet, is a funny fellow. Use your imagination to create a comic character that will delight your audience.

Sheep's Topknot, Ears, and Tail

For the topknot, glue clumps of fiberfill or cotton balls to a child-size headband.

For the ears, cut ear shapes from poster board. Color the center of the ears pink, and then glue fiberfill or cotton balls to the outside of each ear. Tape the ears to the headband or to barrettes.

For the tail, cut a tail shape from poster board. Glue fiberfill or cotton balls to the tail. Use duct tape to secure the tail to the back of the child's waistband or belt.

Donkey's Mane, Ears, and Tail

For the donkey's mane, fold lengthwise a piece of gray or brown construction paper. Along the edge of the paper that's opposite the fold, make three-inch parallel cuts through both thicknesses of paper to create a fringe. Tape the mane to the top of the child's shirt.

For the donkey's ears, cut out ear shapes from gray or brown poster board. Tape the ears to a headband or to barrettes. You can tape the ears pointing up or down, or you can fold one ear for a lopsided look.

For the donkey's tail, fray the last four inches of a twelve- to fifteen-inch length of rope. Tie the unfrayed end of the tail to the back of a child's belt.

Angel's Gown and Halo

For the Angel's gown, fold a bedsheet in half. Cut a hole in the center large enough for a head to fit through. Use a white belt or tie to go under the back side of the sheet and around the front side; then tie the tie. Trim the Angel of the Lord's gown with gold garland or glitter glue.

For the Angel's halo, use a small foam wreath shape that will fit on a child's head. Wrap silver garland around the wreath. Wrap gold garland around the Angel of the Lord's halo.

Virtual Reality Spectacles (VRS)

Photocopy the VRS pattern on to poster board and cut it out. Ask a child to decorate it. Attach the VRS to an ordinary pair of sunglasses.

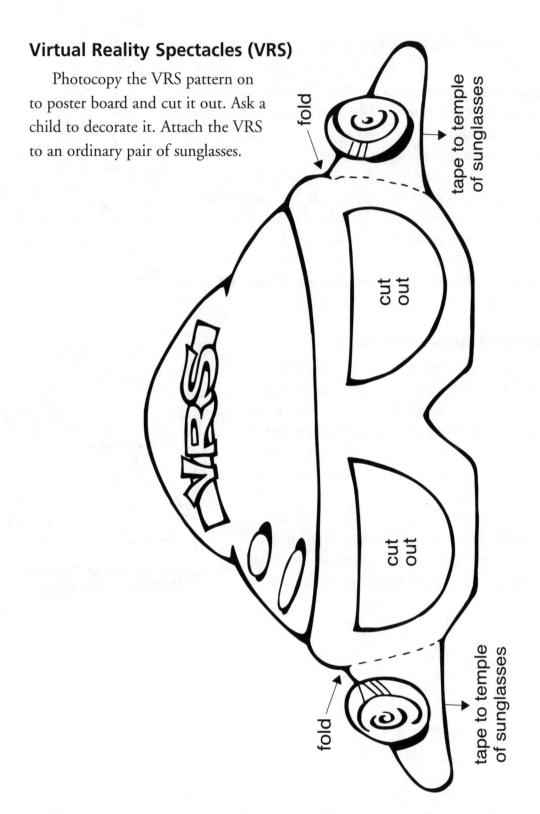

Caspar's Crown

Photocopy the pattern onto poster board and cut it out. Ask a child to decorate it with glitter glue or brightly colored markers. Attach a strip of paper to make the crown fit the child's head.

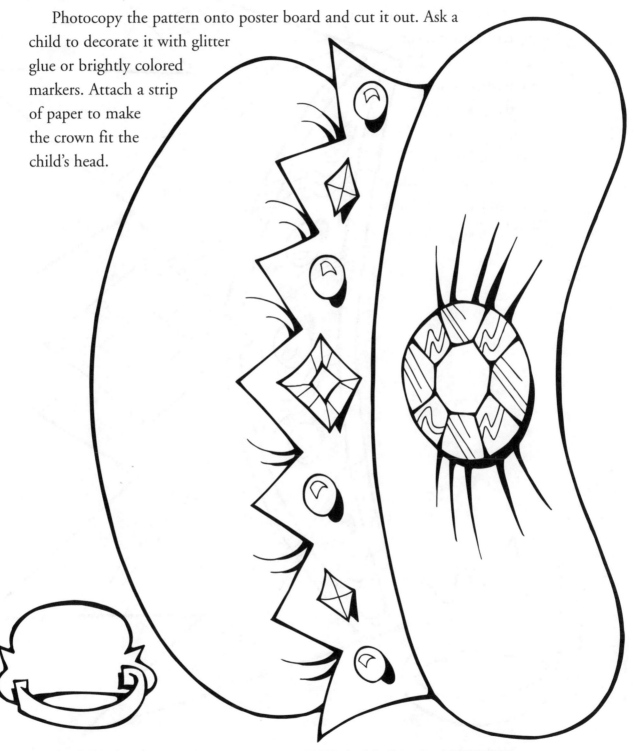

Melchior's Crown

Photocopy the pattern onto poster board and cut it out. Ask a child to decorate it with glitter glue or brightly colored markers. Attach a strip of paper to make the crown fit the child's head.

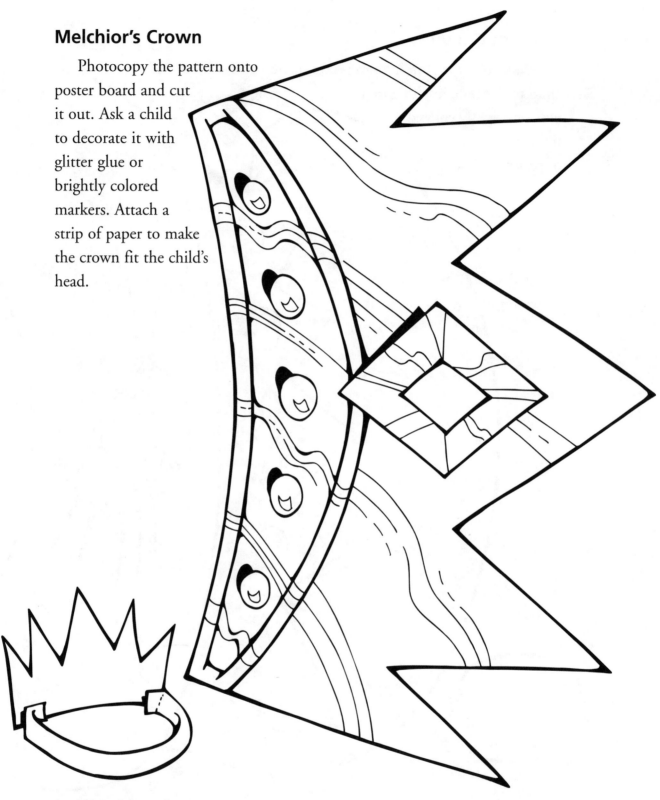

Balthazar's Crown

Photocopy the pattern onto poster board and cut it out. Ask a child to decorate it with glitter glue or brightly colored markers. Attach a strip of paper to make the crown fit the child's head.

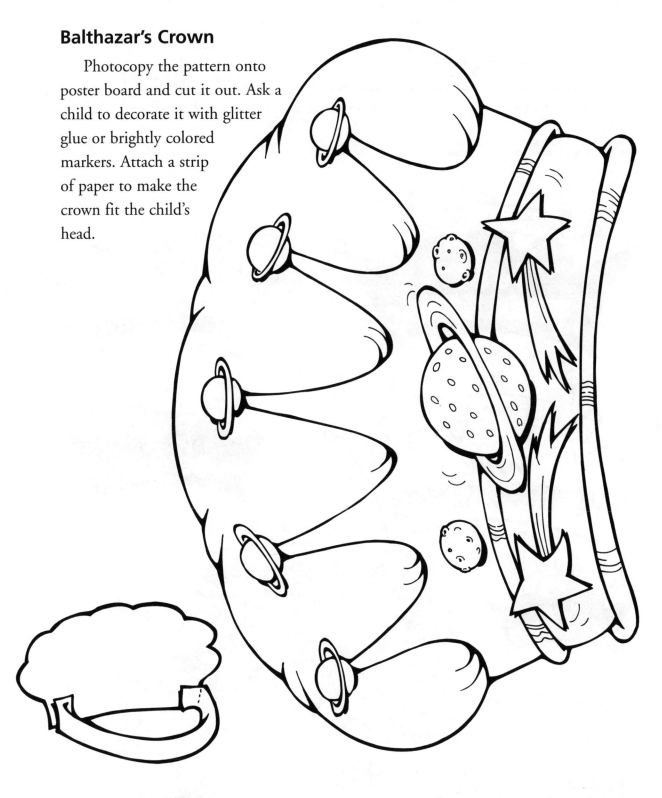

PUBLICIZING
the Pageant

Assign an older student the responsibility of getting the word out! Have kids help add the appropriate performance information to the flier (p. 17) and photocopy it to use as bulletin inserts and fliers. Or enlarge individual pieces of the clip art on a photocopier, and use the clip art on posters that the children design. Kids can also use a computer with CD-ROM capability to print out the clip art from the CD. They'll enjoy e-mailing the pageant publicity pieces to friends.

Date: _____

Time: _____

Place: _____

SETTING THE STAGE
Props and All

Work as a team to set up the stage. Use the following instructions to help you. The stage can be as simple or as elaborate as you and your cast desire. You can adjust the location of props according to the space available. If space is restricted, move the props to either stage left or stage right after a scene has ended to make room for the next scene. This would allow each scene to take place center stage.

● Manger scene—Scatter straw or shredded paper on the floor. Make a rustic-looking manger using a crate or box. Put straw or shredded paper into the manger, trailing out so that it's visible to the audience. The small doll with a blanket is hidden inside the manger. Set Mary's wooden stool next to the manger. Keep the manger scene darkened until its spotlight cue is indicated in the script.

● Shepherds' field—Set a few artificial plants adjacent to poster board green hills as a backdrop with stars hanging down from the night sky. Keep the Shepherds' field darkened until its spotlight cue is indicated in the script.

● Herod's Court—Place an old armchair (must have arms) covered with a regal-looking sheet at center stage. If you like, Servants can hold up sheets attached to dowels to frame Herod's throne.

● House scene—Put a wooden chair on stage for Mary to sit on next to a small wooden table with a simple vase and flowers. Hang a large poster board star above the scene.

WEE THREE KINGS
The Script

Use this script to familiarize yourself with the dialogue and actions in *Wee Three Kings*. Remember, kids don't have to memorize the lines or even lip-sync the words. As they rehearse, encourage kids to come up with their own ideas and actions. Incorporate their ideas into the pageant as much as possible.

Some staging terms are used in this script. "Downstage" is toward the front of the stage, the area closest to the audience. "Upstage" is toward the back of the stage. "Stage left" is the left side of the stage as you face the audience. "Stage right" is the right side of the stage as you face the audience. "Center stage" is the middle section of the stage.

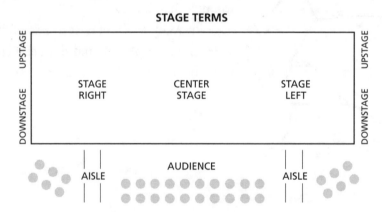

Photocopy the Christmas hymns (p. 48), and pass out copies at the beginning of the pageant. Appoint someone to introduce the pageant and to invite the audience to sing along during the program.

THE PAGEANT

Before the pageant begins, set the time machine center stage with the throne hidden behind it. Set the manger scene stage right and the Shepherds' field stage left. The scrolls are set offstage right, where the Roman Soldier and the Scribes can pick them up as they enter. Gert and Ernie are in the time machine. Gert has the VRS tucked into the neckline of her T-shirt.

ACTIONS	WORDS
(1) Stage is darkened. Light and smoke are coming from the time machine. GERT and ERNIE fall out of either side of the box and land sitting up. GERT is stage left of the box.	

ERNIE

ACTIONS	WORDS
BOTH stand up and dust themselves off. ERNIE points at GERT.	Gertrude Allison Gordon! You are *soo* in trouble! I told you not to mess with the controls!

GERT

ACTIONS	WORDS
They walk around in front of the time machine, facing each other accusingly.	Stick a sock in it, Ernie! Besides, I didn't mean to! I accidentally bumped the enter key.

ERNIE

ACTIONS	WORDS
ERNIE slaps forehead, then shakes head in disbelief.	Like you *accidentally* booted up the time-travel program and *accidentally* set it for who knows when and who knows where?

GERT

ACTIONS	WORDS
GERT waves him away with both hands.	Ah, quit your whining and help me figure out what to do. If we find out where we are, we can reverse what we did...

ERNIE

ACTIONS	WORDS
ERNIE points to himself, then to GERT.	What *we* did? You mean what *you* did. You're the one that's always gettin' us into trouble!

GERT

ACTIONS	WORDS
GERT haughtily moves shoulders back and forth, nose in the air. On "remember," she points to head.	We aren't in trouble. Mom and Dad won't ever find out. Remember, this is a *time* machine. We can get back even before we left!

ACTIONS	WORDS

ERNIE

ERNIE hangs head, then shakes index finger at GERT. He tilts head from side to side.	OK, I'll help, but it's still all your fault! What do you want me to do?

GERT

GERT holds up index finger.	First, we need to find out where we are and what year we're in. We've got to know that so we can program the machine's computer.

ERNIE

ERNIE looks around.	It's too dark to go exploring.

GERT

GERT makes a "come along" wave with one hand.	Let's check the readouts and see if they give us a clue.
Both go to GERT'S side of time machine and stick their heads inside. RACHEL and CALEB enter stealthily from stage left, crouch, and listen.	

ERNIE

ERNIE pulls head out of time machine, then shakes his head.	I don't see anything that's helpful.

GERT

GERT pulls her head out of the time machine, then scratches her head.	You're right, Ernie. The time readout has changed to Roman numerals. I can't remember how to read them.

ACTIONS	WORDS

ERNIE

ERNIE shrugs shoulders.	It's all Greek to me.

GERT

GERT playfully pushes ERNIE'S shoulder.	You mean "geek," don't you? Just like you?

ERNIE

ERNIE pushes back, his voice rising.	Hey, stop pushing!

GERT

GERT pushes ERNIE again.	Hey, yourself!

RACHEL and CALEB step forward to intervene.	

CALEB

CALEB puts index finger over lips.	Shh! You'll wake the guards.

RACHEL

RACHEL pats the air with both hands in front of her, palms down.	Yes, please be quiet. Our masters will be in a foul mood if they wake up too early.

ERNIE

ERNIE puts hand on chest.	I'm sorry! We didn't know anyone was around.

GERT

GERT stands with hands on hips.	Who are you?

ACTIONS	WORDS

CALEB

CALEB replies with pride, his shoulders back and chin held high. On "my sister," he points to RACHEL with open hand.	My name is Caleb and this is my sister Rachel. We are servants in the court of King Herod, ruler of Judea.

GERT & ERNIE TOGETHER

GERT and ERNIE look at each other with surprise.	King Herod?

CALEB

CALEB continues to stand straight and speak with pride.	That's right. We are entrusted with cleaning the royal chamber pots as well as carrying water for the royal kitchens.

GERT

GERT tilts head.	Is this the King Herod from the Bible?

RACHEL & CALEB TOGETHER

RACHEL and CALEB look at each other.	Bible?

GERT

GERT waves them away.	*(Impatiently)* Never mind. It's too hard to explain right now.

CALEB

CALEB makes "come along" gesture.	Someone's coming. Quick, we've got to hide this strange little house and find you some normal clothes.

ACTIONS	WORDS

CALEB

CALEB starts pushing time machine toward stage left. On "Help me!" he looks back at the others. Then together the four move time machine off stage.	**Help me!**

SERVANT 1

	(*Offstage*) **Hurry, you heard the gong!**

SERVANT 2

	(*Offstage*) **He'll be angry if you're late.**

SERVANT 3

	(*Offstage*) **What's the fuss? Why do we have to get up so early?**

3

Several servants rush on from stage right. They line up at an angle across the stage, standing at attention, facing the audience. AHAB follows, strutting back and forth in front of them as he speaks. The JESTER follows AHAB and imitates his strutting while the hand puppet, YUK, mouths AHAB'S words.	

AHAB

AHAB holds hands behind back. He points at SERVANT 1 on "Are the pomegranates..."	(*Demanding respect*) **You all know that we are expecting three very important foreign dignitaries. Everything must be perfect! Are the pomegranates and figs prepared?**

ACTIONS	WORDS

YUK

SERVANT 1 nods. SERVANTS try to hide their snickering.	They've been rehearsing all night, sir.

AHAB

AHAB points at SERVANT 2.	Have you gathered the nuts?

YUK

SERVANT 2 nods. SERVANTS snicker more loudly.	We're all here, sir.

AHAB

AHAB turns and points to YUK and then points offstage.	(*Threatening*) Begone, you bag of camel slobber! And take the Jester with you before you both feel my lash!
JESTER and YUK exit stage right.	

AHAB

AHAB faces SERVANTS sternly.	(*Sternly*) Have the water jars all been filled?
The SERVANTS look at each other, realizing that RACHEL and CALEB are absent.	

AHAB

On "You!" AHAB points to SERVANT 3. AHAB shakes his fist at the SERVANTS and then points offstage.	Where are the two water bearers? (*Losing patience*) You! Find them immediately. If they are not here when the gong sounds again, you will all suffer my whip. Now, all of you, *go!*

ACTIONS	WORDS
4 SERVANTS run off stage in both directions. AHAB exits stage right. The four children enter stage left. GERT and ERNIE have changed into Bible-times apparel, but GERT still has the VRS tucked into the neckline of her tunic.	

CALEB

CALEB wipes his brow.	**Phew, that was close!**

GERT

GERT grimaces.	**That was the meanest guy I've ever seen. What a grouch!**

CALEB

On "clothes," CALEB lifts ERNIE'S tunic slightly and points to ERNIE'S jeans.	**Ahab is short-tempered. Who do you serve and where do you come from? I've never seen clothes like yours before.**

GERT

GERT scratches her head, puzzled.	*(Hesitating)* **It's kinda hard to explain. We came from another time in that machine you saw.**

CALEB

	Does your master own the machine?

GERT

GERT folds her arms across her chest indignantly.	*(Indignantly)* **We don't have a master. We're not servants. Our parents invented the machine.**

ACTIONS	WORDS

ERNIE

ERNIE tugs at GERT'S sleeve impatiently.	*(Impatiently)* **And we've got to get back home right away. I need to go to school!**

RACHEL

With wide-eyed surprise, RACHEL grasps GERT by both arms.	**You go to school? Are you training to become scribes?**

GERT

GERT shakes her head.	**No. Back home all the kids have to go to school.**

RACHEL

RACHEL turns to audience, focusing "far away."	**Oh, how I wish I could go to school.**

CALEB

CALEB pretends to carry a heavy bucket in each hand.	*(With pretended strain in voice)* **It sure would be easier than carrying jars full of water all day.**

RACHEL

RACHEL points to the hem of GERT'S jeans.	**Does everybody wear clothes like that where you come from? What do you call those things that cover your legs?**

ERNIE

ERNIE pulls up the hem of his tunic and sticks one leg out.	**They're called jeans. Everybody wears them.**

ACTIONS	WORDS

GERT

GERT stands with hands on hips. Then she drops her hands and turns to CALEB.	OK, Ernie. But we've got some important things we need to find out. Caleb, do you know what year this is?

CALEB

CALEB stands proudly with his hands behind his back.	This is the thirty-first year that Augustus has been the emperor.

GERT

GERT throws her arms up in frustration.	*(Frustrated)* Duh! How is that supposed to help?

ERNIE

ERNIE takes GERT'S wrists and gently draws them down. He holds up index finger and recites the Scripture from memory.	But it does, Gert. Remember in the Christmas story when Mary and Joseph went to be taxed? It says, *(reciting from memory)* "In those days Caesar Augustus issued a decree that a census should be taken of the entire Roman world."
On "we," he points back and forth between himself and GERT.	*(Excitedly)* Gert, we must be in the court of the King Herod, the one who was visited by the wise men!

CALEB

CALEB grabs ERNIE'S arm.	What's this "Christmas story"? Can you tell it to us?

ERNIE

ERNIE snaps his fingers in an "aw-phooey" gesture.	I wish I had my virtual reality specs with me. My VRS had a Christmas scene in its memory.

5

ACTIONS	WORDS
GERT takes VRS off neck of tunic, holds them up, and clears throat several times with increasing impatience.	

ERNIE

ERNIE claps hands to the sides of his head and looks up at ceiling. He looks down just before he says "Gert!" Then he points to GERT with both index fingers.	**Then you could see for yourselves.** *(Whining)* **Oh, I wish I hadn't left them back home. They make everything look so real, as if you're right there. I've had them since...Gert! You've got your VRS?**

GERT

GERT polishes VRS lenses on sleeve of tunic.	**I never go anywhere without these puppies!**

ERNIE

ERNIE jumps up and down eagerly. GERT puts on VRS and presses imaginary buttons on the temples.	*(Excitedly)* **What're you waitin' for? Boot 'em up: Bible program...** *(pauses)* **New Testament...** *(pauses)* **Gospel of Luke...** *(pauses)* **Chapter 2.**

GERT

	OK. We're set.

ERNIE

ERNIE takes VRS off GERT and puts them on CALEB.	**Here, Caleb, now you can see what I was talking about.**

CALEB

CALEB steps back in alarm, then takes VRS off and hands them back to ERNIE.	*(Frightened)* **Help! Help! What have you done to me?**

ACTIONS	WORDS

GERT

GERT looks up at ceiling, palms up in exasperation.	**Chill out, kid. Where we come from people watch these all the time.**

ERNIE

ERNIE tries to give VRS back to CALEB, but CALEB pushes them away.	**Yeah, come on, Caleb. Try 'em. They won't hurt you.**

RACHEL

RACHEL reaches out for VRS.	**I'll try.**

CALEB

CALEB brushes RACHEL aside and puts VRS on to "view" ROMAN SOLDIER and manger scene.	*(Not to be upstaged by his little sister)* **No, he asked me. I can do it.**

ROMAN SOLDIER

☀ **6** SPOTLIGHT moves to ROMAN SOLDIER. ROMAN SOLDIER enters stage right and mimes reading from scroll. MARY, JOSEPH, and DONKEY enter stage left and walk slowly to stage right. MARY sits on stool by manger.	**"In those days Caesar Augustus issued a decree that a census should be taken of the entire Roman world...And everyone went to his own town to register. So Joseph also went up from the town of Nazareth in Galilee to Judea, to Bethlehem the town of David, because he belonged to the house and line of David. He went there to register with Mary, who was pledged to be married to him and was expecting a child."**
☀ **7** SPOTLIGHT moves to manger scene. ROMAN SOLDIER exits stage right.	**SONG: "O Little Town of Bethlehem"**

ACTIONS	WORDS

NARRATOR'S VOICE

8 MARY picks up small doll from manger, rearranges blanket around it, then returns doll to manger.

Offstage) **"While they were there, the time came for the baby to be born, and she gave birth to her firstborn, a son. She wrapped him in cloths and placed him in a manger, because there was no room for them in the inn."**

9 During the song, SHEPHERDS and SHEEP enter stage left and remain in the Shepherd's field. One SHEPHERD sits and the others lean against their crooks.

SONG: "Away in a Manger"

NARRATOR'S VOICE

10 SPOTLIGHT shifts from manger scene to SHEPHERDS.
CALEB hands VRS to RACHEL, who puts them on. She looks toward SHEPHERDS and watches their actions. ANGEL OF THE LORD enters and stands upstage of SHEEP and SHEPHERDS. SHEPHERDS hold arms over faces, fall to knees, and cover heads. ANGEL OF THE LORD reaches out slowly toward SHEPHERDS. ANGEL OF THE LORD points toward manger scene.
ANGELS run on stage and form a semicircle behind the ANGEL OF THE LORD, facing the SHEPHERDS, who look up and around at the ANGELS.

(Offstage) **"And there were shepherds living out in the fields nearby, keeping watch over their flocks at night. An angel of the Lord appeared to them, and the glory of the Lord shone around them, and they were terrified. But the angel said to them, 'Do not be afraid. I bring you good news of great joy that will be for all the people. Today in the town of David a Savior has been born to you; he is Christ the Lord. This will be a sign to you: You will find a baby wrapped in cloths and lying in a manger.' Suddenly a great company of the heavenly host appeared with the angel, praising God and saying, 'Glory to God in the highest, and on earth peace to men on whom his favor rests.' "**

11

SONG: "Angels We Have Heard on High"

ACTIONS	WORDS

NARRATOR'S VOICE

 ANGEL OF THE LORD and ANGELS run offstage. SHEPHERDS stand and converse.

 SPOTLIGHT follows as SHEPHERDS walk across stage to manger scene. SHEEP exit stage left.

SHEPHERDS kneel before manger.

(Offstage) **"When the angels had left them and gone into heaven, the shepherds said to one another, 'Let's go to Bethlehem and see this thing that has happened, which the Lord has told us about.' So they hurried off and found Mary and Joseph, and the baby, who was lying in the manger."**

 SPOTLIGHT on children. Manger scene participants exit right, taking manger and stool. RACHEL removes VRS and returns them to GERT, who hangs them on the neckline of her tunic.

RACHEL

 RACHEL crosses hands over heart.

What a beautiful story—a Savior, born in Bethlehem.

CALEB

On "dirty," CALEB pinches his nose as if disgusted.

But in a shabby old stable? And in Bethlehem? I've been there. Bethlehem's just a dirty peasant village.

RACHEL

RACHEL drops one hand from over her heart and lets it fall to her side.

And this baby was so poor! Even poorer than we are.

ACTIONS	WORDS

CALEB

CALEB stands with his fists on his hips, shoulders back and feet well apart.	We aren't poor. We live in the court of King Herod.

RACHEL

RACHEL grasps her armband.	But we don't own anything, not even ourselves. The armbands we wear show that Herod owns us.

CALEB

CALEB grabs GERT'S hand and RACHEL grabs ERNIE'S hand to help them line up with SERVANTS. GERT holds VRS behind back.	Quick, here comes Ahab! Get in line and try to act like you belong.
SERVANTS and JESTER with YUK rush in from both stage right and left and line up at an angle, center stage. JESTER is closest to audience. AHAB follows, holds hands behind his back, and addresses SERVANTS.	

AHAB

On "here," AHAB points straight down.	I've finished my inspection and the palace is ready. You are all to remain here to do our master's bidding.

YUK

	And what am I bid for this fine lot of losers?

ACTIONS	WORDS
Enter KING HEROD and COURTIERS stage right. HEROD sits on throne center stage while others line up opposite SERVANTS. Two SERVANTS move, one on either side of throne.	

HERALD

ACTIONS	WORDS
(14) HERALD enters stage right and stands at attention.	**The distinguished ambassadors of Persia: Caspar, Melchior, and Balthazar.**

HEROD

ACTIONS	WORDS
WISE MEN enter stage right and stand downstage and to right of throne. HEROD holds hand out toward WISE MEN, palm up.	*(Ingratiating)* **We welcome our esteemed Eastern visitors.**

YUK

ACTIONS	WORDS
Aside to audience. SERVANTS snicker.	**What do they have to be "steamed" about?**

HEROD

ACTIONS	WORDS
HEROD draws his hand to his chest.	**How may our humble kingdom serve you?**

YUK

ACTIONS	WORDS
After "onions," SERVANTS put hands over mouths to keep from laughing.	**Three camel burgers to go—light mayo, hold the onions.**

CASPAR

ACTIONS	WORDS
CASPAR looks back toward entrance, then sweeps hand from entrance to himself.	*(Commanding but polite)* **We have come a great distance in search of a child. Where is he that is born King of the Jews?**

ACTIONS	WORDS

GERT & ERNIE

GERT and ERNIE point at each other, then whisper excitedly together.	*(Whispering)* **For we have seen his star...**

MELCHIOR

MELCHIOR points up.	**For we have seen his star in the East and have come to worship him.**

HEROD

A buzzing is heard among the court. HEROD grabs arms of throne and sits up straight. Then he sits back, pretending to relax.	*(Upset, but trying to maintain cool)* **You have come to the right place. If you will excuse me, I will meet with my advisers and then send for you...**

YUK

Aside to audience.	**...when I figure out what in the world's going on.**

CASPAR

CASPAR nods.	**Very well. We will await your summons.**

The WISE MEN bow slightly and exit stage left.	

HEROD

15 SCRIBES enter stage right.	**Scribes!**

ACTIONS	WORDS

COURTIERS

COURTIERS turn to each other. Some grasp a shoulder, others put their hands beside their mouths as if whispering.	*(Whispering)* **A new king!...This can't be good news for us!...What does this mean?**

HEROD

HEROD pounds hands on arms of throne, then "tents" his fingers. Points to SCRIBES	**Silence!** *(Maliciously)* **We must put down this upstart immediately...but quietly. These things must be done delicately.** *(Pauses.)* **Scribes, what is written about these matters?**

SCRIBE 1

SCRIBES step to the throne, unrolling scrolls and searching through them, flustered. SCRIBE 1 holds the scroll with one hand and points with the other.	*(Upset, confused)* **Here, your majesty...Oh no, that's not right.**

SCRIBE 2

SCRIBE 2 points upward, arm at full length. He mumbles while reading.	**I have it! Brought...king...no, no.**

OLD SCRIBE

OLD SCRIBE approaches throne and bows head. On the words "But you," he draws himself up straight, reciting Scripture from memory.	**Sire, ancient Hebrew Scriptures tell of a promised Messiah who will rule with justice and peace. The prophet Micah names his birthplace: "But you, Bethlehem Ephrathah, though you are small among the clans of Judah, out of you will come for me one who will be ruler over Israel."**

ACTIONS	WORDS

HEROD

HEROD strokes his chin, musing.	Bethlehem. Not far away. Hmm. Maybe these Persian sandal slurpers can be of service to me. Herald, summon our visitors to meet me here alone at the sixth hour.
All exit stage right except the four children.	

CALEB

CALEB steps back from GERT and ERNIE with his hand up in front of him in a protective gesture.	*(Fearfully)* **You knew what those men were going to say before they even said it!**

ERNIE

ERNIE faces CALEB	*(Gently)* **Those words are part of the holy writings about Jesus. Those visitors are the wise men.**

RACHEL

RACHEL faces ERNIE.	**Wise men? What makes them wise?**

ERNIE

ERNIE taps the side of his head with his index finger.	**They were wise enough to recognize God's Son, even though he came as a helpless baby born in a lowly stable.**

GERT

GERT jumps up and down excitedly.	*(Excited)* **Why don't we follow the wise men to Bethlehem? OK?**

ACTIONS	WORDS

ERNIE

| ERNIE gives GERT a high five. | OK, Gert! |

GERT

| GERT returns VRS to the neckline of tunic and extends hand, palm up. | How about you, Rachel and Caleb? |

RACHEL

| RACHEL nods her head, but CALEB shakes his head. | What's the matter, Caleb? |

CALEB

| CALEB shakes his head sadly. Then he points defiantly at RACHEL. | I can't go with you. My duty is to King Herod. And yours should be, too! |

RACHEL

| RACHEL shakes head emphatically. | *(Determined)* I must go to see this child King. |

CALEB

| CALEB takes RACHEL by the shoulders and shakes her slightly. | *(Pleading)* What if you get caught? Herod will treat you as a traitor. Then no one can save you! |

RACHEL

| | Gert and Ernie believe this child is God's own Son. That makes him more important than my duty to Herod or anyone. |

ACTIONS	WORDS
## GERT	
GERT stands with her hands on her hips.	*(Demanding)* **Who are you going to serve, Caleb? King Herod or God?**
## CALEB	
CALEB stomps off stage left.	**I'm going straight to the king and tell him what you three are plotting!**
## GERT	
GERT holds her hands palms up, shoulder high with elbows bent and tight to her body.	**Rachel, what do we do now? When he tells Herod, it'll be very bad for you!**
## ERNIE	
ERNIE hangs head, shaking it slowly. On "I've got to go..." he lifts his head and looks at GERT.	**If Caleb only knew what Herod is *really* planning to do. I've got to go tell Caleb!**
## RACHEL	
RACHEL reaches out to hold ERNIE back.	**You'll be putting yourself in great danger!**
## ERNIE	
	(Decisively) **God will take care of me. You two go on to Bethlehem, and I'll meet you there.**
## GERT	
GERT pats ERNIE on his head.	*(Somewhat tenderly)* **Be careful! You're the only little brother I've got.**
ERNIE exits stage left.	

ACTIONS	WORDS
## RACHEL	
RACHEL tugs on GERT'S sleeve.	**Someone's coming! Hurry! Let's go!**
They exit together down aisle.	
HEROD enters stage right, looks around suspiciously, then takes a seat on his throne. The WISE MEN enter and stand to the side.	
## HEROD	
HEROD folds his arms across his chest. On "When" he leans toward WISE MEN.	**My advisers have searched carefully for the answer to your question, but first I have a question for you. When did this star first appear?**
## CASPAR	
CASPAR motions toward BALTHAZAR with his open hand.	**Balthazar would be the one to answer that question.**
## BALTHAZAR	
BALTHAZAR shades eyes with hand.	**Saw it first, I did. Yes!**
## HEROD	
	When did you see it?
## BALTHAZAR	
BALTHAZAR turns around in a circle, still shading eyes.	**In the western sky, it was.**

17

41

ACTIONS	WORDS

HEROD

On "when," HEROD pounds fist into palm of hand.	*(Losing patience)* **But *when* did you see it?**

BALTHAZAR

BALTHAZAR counts to six on his fingers.	**Six months before our trip we started.**

HEROD

HEROD tilts head back and rolls eyes toward ceiling.	**And when did you start your trip?**

BALTHAZAR

BALTHAZAR scratches his head. On "one year," he holds up index finger, then shakes head.	**Years it seems ago. So long traveling we have been. But only one year it may be. Certain I am not.**

HEROD

HEROD grows increasingly frustrated.	**So it might have been one or two years ago?**

MELCHIOR

MELCHIOR nods his head and gently puts an arm on BALTHAZAR'S shoulder.	**Yes, we've been traveling about a year and a half.**

HEROD

HEROD sits back in throne. He puts hand over heart on "me." He leans forward, hand still on his heart. He points up on "Perhaps" and then "tents" his fingers.	**You've come a great distance seeking this child. I'm pleased you have brought your questions to me so that I, too, may honor him. Unfortunately, my duties keep me from traveling with you just now. Perhaps you will do me this kindness. Go and search diligently**

ACTIONS	WORDS
	for the young child; and when you have found him, bring me word again, that I may come and worship him also.

CASPAR

ACTIONS	WORDS
The WISE MEN bow with a flourish.	We will do so if the heavens allow.

HEROD

ACTIONS	WORDS
HEROD slaps his thigh and rises from throne. He puts his arms on shoulders of two WISE MEN. They all exit stage left while HEROD continues.	It's settled then. *(Pauses.)* And now, will you join me in the royal banquet hall? *(Pauses.)* You'll stay the night, of course. I've had rooms prepared for you.

 Turn off SPOTLIGHT.

18 Banquet commotion is heard from offstage. Throne is removed from stage.

 Turn on SPOTLIGHT.
WISE MEN enter stage left. They are carrying their robes and blankets and are clad only in tunics. They yawn sleepily, spread out blankets, and lie down on them. Soon BALTHAZAR is heard snoring.
Following "dream" music, WISE MEN wake, stretch, get up, and begin to put robes back on.

BALTHAZAR

ACTIONS	WORDS
BALTHAZAR touches his head and spirals his finger upward.	Last night the strangest dream I had!

CASPAR

ACTIONS	WORDS
CASPAR points upward.	I, too, dreamed.

ACTIONS	WORDS

MELCHIOR

MELCHIOR points upward. On "voice," he cups his hand behind his ear.	**As did I. I heard a voice warning me to return home by another way.**

CASPAR

CASPAR points upward again.	**I had the same dream!**

BALTHAZAR

BALTHAZAR cups his hand behind his ear.	**Heard the same thing, did I. A message from God, must it be?**

CASPAR

CASPAR nods his head emphatically.	**Indeed!**

MELCHIOR

MELCHIOR quickly gathers up blankets. WISE MEN exit down aisle. SPOTLIGHT is turned off.	**Let's leave this place quickly, never to return.**
With stage darkened, set up house scene. MARY sits in chair, and JOSEPH stands behind her. Both MARY and JOSEPH gaze lovingly at larger doll in MARY'S arms.	
19 SPOTLIGHT moves with WISE MEN as they enter and point at star. They proceed with gifts up the aisle toward house scene. GERT and RACHEL are creeping up the aisle, following WISE MEN at a distance.	**SONG: "We Three Kings of Orient Are"**

ACTIONS	WORDS
## RACHEL	
RACHEL cups hands to mouth and whispers.	*(Whispering)* **Where are we?**
## GERT	
GERT turns head from side to side, looking around.	*(Whispering)* **This must be the place.** *(Relieved)* **We've made it, and still no sign of Herod's soldiers.**
## RACHEL	
RACHEL tugs on GERT'S sleeve.	**What's happening?**
## GERT	
GERT points toward house scene.	*(With awe)* **The wise men found him.**
## NARRATOR'S VOICE	
The WISE MEN kneel left of MARY and present their gifts during Scripture reading.	*(Offstage)* **"On coming to the house, they saw the child with his mother Mary, and they bowed down and worshiped him. Then they opened their treasures and presented him with gifts of gold and of incense and of myrrh."**
RACHEL and GERT move slowly to the stage and stand right of MARY. CALEB enters from stage right, with ERNIE directly behind him.	
## CALEB	
CALEB reaches toward RACHEL, but is too far away to touch her.	**Rachel!**

20

ACTIONS	WORDS

GERT

RACHEL and GERT whirl around to face him, showing fear. GERT shades her eyes to see CALEB in the dark.	*(Demanding)* **So you found us. Did you bring the soldiers with you?**

ERNIE

ERNIE steps out from behind CALEB.	**It's all right. It's just us.**

CALEB

RACHEL steps toward CALEB.	**I've come to join you.**

RACHEL

	What made you change your mind?

CALEB

CALEB points back over his shoulder with his thumb.	**He's a monster!**

RACHEL

RACHEL puts her hand on CALEB'S shoulder.	**Who? What do you mean?**

CALEB

CALEB makes "claws" of his fingers and draws them down both sides of his face. He hangs his head in shame.	**Herod! He's a vicious monster! We overheard his cruel plans for this innocent Child. I couldn't stay at the palace any longer.** *(Ashamed)* **Can you ever forgive me?**

RACHEL

In answer, RACHEL hugs CALEB. She takes him by the hand.	**Come, see the Son of God.**

ACTIONS	WORDS
21 RACHEL leads all the children closer to JOSEPH and MARY. MARY begins to rock the doll to sleep in her arms.	SONG: "Silent Night"

RACHEL

ACTIONS	WORDS
22 Taking off her armband, RACHEL speaks.	Wherever I go, from now on I'll be serving the King of kings.
CALEB hesitates a moment, then takes off his own armband. He and RACHEL move forward, kneel beside WISE MEN, and present their armbands. GERT takes the VRS from the neck of her tunic and starts forward.	

ERNIE

ACTIONS	WORDS
ERNIE puts his hand on the back of GERT'S shoulder.	Wait, Gert, I don't have a gift for Jesus!

GERT

ACTIONS	WORDS
GERT puts arm on ERNIE'S shoulder.	*(Encouragingly, with pride)* Well, duh, little brother! You knew God wanted you to help Caleb, and you were brave enough to do it. Obedience is the best gift anyone could ever give Jesus, the King for all time!
23 GERT and ERNIE move forward and kneel. GERT presents her VRS.	SONG: "O Come All Ye Faithful"

Christmas Hymns
Wee THREE KINGS

We Three Kings of Orient Are

We three kings of Orient are;
Bearing gifts we traverse afar
Field and fountain, moor and
mountain,
Following yonder star.

Chorus:
O star of wonder, star of night,
Star with royal beauty bright,
Westward leading, still proceeding,
Guide us to thy perfect light.

Glorious now behold him arise,
King and God and sacrifice;
"Alleluia, Alleluia!"
Earth to the heav'ns replies.

(Repeat Chorus)

Silent Night

Silent night, holy night,
All is calm, all is bright;
Round yon virgin mother and child,
Holy infant, so tender and mild,
Sleep in heavenly peace,
Sleep in heavenly peace.

Silent night, holy night,
Son of God, love's pure light;
Radiant beams from thy holy face,
With the dawn of redeeming grace,
Jesus, Lord at thy birth,
Jesus, Lord at thy birth.

O Come, All Ye Faithful

O come, all ye faithful, joyful and
triumphant,
O come ye, O come ye to
Bethlehem;
Come and behold him, born the
King of angels.

Chorus:
O come, let us adore him, O come,
let us adore him,
O come, let us adore him, Christ
the Lord.

Sing, choirs of angels, sing in exulta-
tion,
Sing, all yet citizens of heaven above;
Glory to God, in the highest glory.

(Repeat Chorus)

Yea, Lord, we greet thee, born this
happy morning,
Jesus, to thee be all glory given;
Word of the Father, now in flesh
appearing.

(Repeat Chorus)

O Little Town of Bethlehem

O little town of Bethlehem,
How still we see thee lie;
Above thy deep and dreamless sleep
The silent stars go by.
Yet in thy dark streets shineth
The everlasting Light;
The hopes and fears of all the years
Are met in thee tonight.

O holy Child of Bethlehem,
Descend to us, we pray;
Cast out our sin and enter in,
Be born in us today.
We hear the Christmas angels
The great glad tidings tell;
O come to us, abide with us,
Our Lord Emmanuel.

Away in a Manger

Away in a manger, no crib for a bed,
The little Lord Jesus laid down his
sweet head;
The stars in the sky looked down
where he lay,
The little Lord Jesus, asleep on the
hay.

The cattle are lowing, the poor baby
wakes,
But little Lord Jesus, no crying he
makes;
I love thee, Lord Jesus; look down
from the sky,
And stay by my cradle 'til morning
is nigh.

Angels We Have Heard on High

Angels we have heard on high,
Sweetly singing o'er the plains,
And the mountains in reply
Echoing their joyous strains.

Chorus:
Gloria in excelsis Deo!
Gloria in excelsis Deo!

Shepherds, why this jubilee?
Why your joyous strains prolong?
What the gladsome tidings be
Which inspire your heav'nly song?

(Repeat Chorus)